LEGEND

the best of

BOB
MARLEY
and the WAILERS

Photography by Adrian Boot
All photos © Adrian Boot/B.M.M.I. 1995
Except photo on page 42: © David Corio

ISBN 0-7935-3698-7

HAL • LEONARD™
CORPORATION
7777 W. BLUEMOUND RD. P.O. BQX 13819 MILWAUKEE, WI 53213

LEGEND

the best of

BOB MARLEY

and the WAILERS

IS THIS LOVE
Words and Music by Bob Marley

I wanna love you, and treat you right.
I wanna love you, every day and every night.
We'll be together, with a roof right over our heads.
We'll share the shelter of my single bed.
We'll share the same room, Jah provide the bread.

Is this love, is this love,
Is this love, is this love that I'm feelin'?
(Repeat)

I wanna know, wanna know, wanna know now.
I got to know, got to know, got to know now.

I, I'm willing and able,
So I throw my cards on your table.
I wanna love you;
I wanna love you and treat you right.
I wanna love you, every day and every night.
We'll be together, with a roof right over our heads.
We'll share the shelter of my single bed.
We'll share the same room, oh, Jah provide the bread.

Is this love, is this love,
Is this love, is this love that I'm feelin'?
(Repeat)

Oh, yes I know, yes I know, yes I know now. (Repeat)
I, I'm willing and able,
So I throw my cards on your table.
See, I wanna love you,
I wanna love and treat you right,
    love and treat you right.
I wanna love you every day and every night.
We'll be together with a roof right over our heads.
We'll share the shelter of my single bed.
We'll share the same room, Jah provide the bread.
We'll share the shelter of my single bed.

IS THIS LOVE

NO WOMAN NO CRY

Words and Music by Vincent Ford

No woman, no cry. *(4 times)*

'Cause I remember when we used to sit
In the government yard in Trenchtown.
Oba, ob-serving the hypocrites
As they would mingle with the good people we meet;
Good friends we have had, oh good friends we've
    lost along the way.
In this bright future you can't forget your past,
So dry your tears, I say.

No woman, no cry.
No woman, no cry.
Little darlin', don't shed no tears.
No woman, no cry.

Said, said, said I remember when we used to sit
In the government yard in Trenchtown.
And then Georgie would make the fire light,
Log wood burnin' through the night.
Then we would cook corn meal porridge
Of which I'll share with you.

My feet is my only carriage,
So I've got to push on through,
But while I'm gone,...

Ev'rything's gonna be alright. *(7 times)*
Ev'rything's gonna be alright,
So, no woman, no cry.
No, no woman, no woman, no cry.
Oh, little darling, don't shed no tears.
No woman, no cry.

No woman, no woman, no woman, no cry.
No woman, no cry.
Oh, my little darlin', please don't shed no tears.
No woman, no cry, yeah.

No woman, no woman, no cry.

NO WOMAN NO CRY

Words and Music by
VINCENT FORD

Oh, my lit - tle sis - ter

don't shed no tears. ___

No wom - an, no cry.

Guitar solo - ad lib.

Solo ends

D.S. al Coda

COULD YOU BE LOVED

Words and Music by Bob Marley

Could you be loved and be loved? *(Repeat)*

Don't let them fool you
  or even try to school you, oh, no.
We've got a mind of our own.
So, go to hell if what you're thinkin' isn't right.
Love would never leave us alone;
In the darkness there must come out to light.

Could you be loved and be loved? (Repeat)

The road of life is rocky,
  and you may stumble, too.
So while you point your fingers,
  someone else is judgin' you.
Love your brother man.

Could you be, could you be, could you be loved?
Could you be, could you be loved?

Don't let them change you,
  or even rearrange you. Oh, no.
We've got a life to live. Ooh, ooh, ooh.

They say only, only,
  only the fittest of the fittest shall survive.
Stay alive.

Could you be loved and be loved? (Repeat)

You ain't gonna miss your water
  until your well runs dry.
No matter how you treat him,
  the man will never be satisfied.

Could you be, could you be, could you be loved?
Could you be, could you be loved?
(Repeat)

Say somethin', say somethin'. (Repeat)

COULD YOU BE LOVED

Strum Pattern 1
Moderately bright Reggae

Words and Music by
BOB MARLEY

Could you be loved ___

and be loved? ___

Don't let them fool you
Don't let them change you

D.S. al Coda

Could you be, could you be, could you be loved? Could you be, could you be loved?

CODA

Stay a - live oh.

D

Could you be loved

Bm

G

and be loved?

1 D

2 D

You

THREE LITTLE BIRDS

Words and Music by Bob Marley

Don't worry about a thing,
'Cause ev'ry little thing gonna be alright.
Singin', "Don't worry about a thing,
'Cause ev'ry little thing gonna be alright."
Rise up this morning,
*   smiled with the rising sun.*
Three little birds pitch by my doorstep,
*   singin' sweet songs of melodies pure and true,*
Sayin', "This is my message to you-u-u."
Singin'...
(Repeat)

"Don't worry about a thing,
'Cause ev'ry little thing gonna be al-right."
(4 times)

THREE LITTLE BIRDS

Strum Pattern 2
Moderate slow Reggae

Words and Music by
BOB MARLEY

BUFFALO SOLDIER

Words and Music by Bob Marley and Noel George Williams

Buffalo soldier, dreadlock Rasta
There was a buffalo soldier in the heart of America
Stolen from Africa brought to America
Fighting on arrival, fighting for survival; I mean it.
When I analyze the stench
To me it makes a lot of sense
How the dreadlock Rasta was the buffalo soldier.

And he was taken from Africa brought to America
Fighting on arrival, fighting for survival
Said he was a buffalo soldier, dreadlock Rasta.
Buffalo soldier in the heart of America.
If you know your history,
Then you would know where you're coming from
Then you wouldn't have to ask me who the heck do I think I am.

I'm just a buffalo soldier in the heart of America
Stolen from Africa, brought to America
Said he was fighting on arrival, fighting for survival.
Said he was a buffalo soldier, win the war for America.
Singing – wo, yo, yo...

Buffalo soldier trodding through the land
Said you wanna run and then you make a stand
Trodding through the land yeah.
Said he was a buffalo soldier, win the war for America
Buffalo Soldier, dreadlock Rasta.
Fighting on arrival, fighting for survival.
Driven from the mainland to the heart of the Caribbean.
Singing – wo, yo, yo...

Trodding through San Juan in the arms of America
Trodding through Jamaica, the buffalo soldier
Fighting on arrival, fighting for survival
Buffalo soldier, dreadlock Rasta
Wo, yo, yo...

BUFFALO SOLDIER

Words and Music by BOB MARLEY
and NOEL GEORGE WILLIAMS

Buf - fa - lo sol - dier,
tak - en from Af - ri - ca,

dread - lock Ras - ta; There was a buf - fa - lo sol - dier
brought to A - mer - i - ca, fight - ing on ar - riv - al,

in the heart of A - mer - i - ca.
fight - ing for sur - viv - al. Said he was a

34

GET UP STAND UP

Words and Music by Bob Marley

Get up, stand up, stand up for your right. *(3 times)*
Get up, stand up, don't give up the fight.

Preacher man, don't tell me heaven is under the earth.
I know you don't know what life is really worth.
Is not all that glitters is gold and,
    half the story has never been told.
So now you see the light, aay.
Stand up for your right. Come on.

Get up, stand up, stand up for your right.
Get up, stand up, don't give up the fight.
(Repeat)

Most people think great God will come from the sky,
Take away ev'rything, and make ev'rybody feel high.
But if you know what life is worth,
You would look for yours on earth.
And now you see the light.
You stand up for your right, yah!

Get up, stand up, stand up for your right.
Get up, stand up, don't give up the fight.
Get up, stand up. Life is your right,
So we can't give up the fight.
Stand up for your right, Lord, Lord.
Get up, stand up. Keep on struggling on,
Don't give up the fight.

We're sick and tired of your ism and skism game.
Die and go to heaven in Jesus' name, Lord.
We know when we understand.
Almighty God is a living man.
You can fool some people sometimes,
But you can't fool all the people all the time.
So now we see the light.
We gonna stand up for our right.

So you'd better get up, stand up, stand up for your right.
Get up, stand up, don't give up the fight.
Get up, stand up, stand up for your right.
Get up, stand up, don't give up the fight.

GET UP STAND UP

Strum Pattern 2
Moderately slow Reggae

Words and Music by
BOB MARLEY

Get up,　stand up,　don't give up ___ the fight.
Get up,　stand up,　don't give up ___ the fight.
Get up,　stand up,　don't give up ___ the fight.　We're

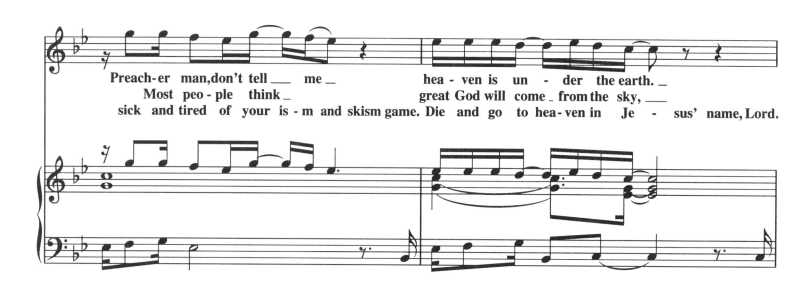

Preach-er man, don't tell ___ me ___　hea - ven is un - der the earth. ___
Most peo - ple think ___　great God will come ___ from the sky, ___
sick and tired of your is - m and skism game. Die and go to hea-ven in Je - sus' name, Lord.

I know you don't ___ know　what ___ life is real - ly worth. ___　Is not all ___
take a - way ev-'ry-thing,　and make ev -'ry-bod - y feel high.　But
We know when we un - der - stand.　Al-might - y God is a liv-ing man. ___ You can fool ___

STIR IT UP

Words and Music by Bob Marley

Stir it up, little darling, stir it up.
Come on, baby, come on and stir it up, little darling, stir it up.
It's been a long, long time since I've got you on my mind.
And now you are here,
I say, it's so clear
To see what we can do, honey, just me and you.

Come on and stir it up, little darling, stir it up.
Come on baby, come on and stir it up, little darling, stir it up.
I'll push the wood, I'll blaze your fire,
Then I'll satisfy your heart's desire.
Said I'll stir it, yeah, ev'ry minute, yeah.
All you got to do is keep it in, baby.
And stir it up, little darling, stir it up.
Come on and stir it up, ooh, little darling, stir it up, yeah.

Oh, will you quench me while I'm thirsty?
Come and cool me down when I'm hot?
Your recipe, darling, is so tasty,
And you sure can stir your pot.
So stir it up, little darling, stir it up.
Come on and stir it up, ooh, little darling, stir it up.
Come on and stir it up, oh, little darling, stir it up.
Stir it up, little darling, stir it up.

(Guitar Solo)

Little darling, stir it up.
Come on and stir it up, little darling, stir it up.

STIR IT UP

Strum Pattern 2
Moderate Reggae

Words and Music by
BOB MARLEY

ONE LOVE

Words and Music by Bob Marley

One love, one heart.
Let's get together and feel all right.
Hear the children crying. (One love.)
Hear the children crying. (One heart.)
Sayin', "Give thanks and praise to the Lord and I will feel all right."
Sayin', "Let's get together and feel all right."
Whoa, whoa, whoa, whoa.

Let them all pass all their dirty remarks. (One love.)
There is one question I'd really love to ask. (One heart.)
Is there a place for the hopeless sinner
Who has hurt all mankind just to save his own?
Believe me.

One love, one heart.
Let's get together and feel all right.
As it was in the beginning, (One love.)
So shall it be in the end. (One heart.)
Alright, "Give thanks and praise to the Lord and I will feel all right."
"Let's get together and feel all right."
One more thing.

Let's get together to fight this Holy Armageddon, (One love.)
So when the Man comes there will be no, no doom. (One song.)
Have pity on those whose chances grow thinner.
There ain't no hiding place from the Father of Creation.

Sayin', "One love, one heart.
Let's get together and feel all right."
I'm pleading to mankind. (One love.)
Oh, Lord. (One heart.) Whoa.

"Give thanks and praise to the Lord and I will feel all right."
Let's get together and feel all right.
(Repeat)

ONE LOVE/PEOPLE GET READY

ONE LOVE
Words and Music by BOB MARLEY
Copyright © 1968
All Rights Controlled by PolyGram International Publishing, Inc.
International Copyright Secured   All Rights Reserved

PEOPLE GET READY
Words and Music by CURTIS MAYFIELD
© 1964 WARNER-TAMERLANE PUBLISHING CORP. (Renewed)
All Rights Reserved

50

51

I SHOT THE SHERIFF

Words and Music by Bob Marley

*I shot the sheriff, but I didn't shoot
no deputy. Oh, no, oh.
I shot the sheriff, but I didn't shoot no
deputy. Ooh, ooh, ooh. Yeah.*

*All around in my hometown
They're tryin' to track me down, yeah.
They say they want to bring me in
guilty
For the killing of a deputy, for the life
of a deputy.
But I say, oh, now, now...*

*Oh, I shot the sheriff, but I swear it was
in self defense. Ooh, ooh, ooh.
I said, I shot the sheriff, Oh Lord,
And they say it is a capital offense. Ooh,
ooh, ooh. Hear this.*

*Sheriff John Brown always hated me;
For what, I don't know.
Ev'ry time I plant a seed,
He said, "Kill it before it grows."
He said, "Kill them before they grow."*

*And so, oh, now, now,
Read it in the news.*

*I shot the sheriff, but I swear it was in
self defense. Ooh, ooh, ooh. Where
was the deputy?
I said, I shot the sheriff, but I swear it
was in self defense.*

*Freedom came my way one day,
And I started out of town, yeah!
All of a sudden I saw Sheriff John Brown
Aiming to shoot me down.
So I shot, I shot, I shot him down.
And I say, if I am guilty I will pay.*

*I shot the sheriff, but I say, but I didn't
shoot no deputy. Oh, no, oh.
I shot the sheriff, but I didn't shoot no
deputy. Ooo, ooo, ooh.*

*Reflexes had the better of me.
And what is to be must be.
Ev'ry day the bucket a-go-a well;*

*One day the bottom a-go drop out.
One day the bottom a-go drop out.
I say, I, I, ...*

*I, I shot the sheriff, but I didn't shoot
the deputy, no.
(Repeat)*

I SHOT THE SHERIFF

Words and Music by
BOB MARLEY

WAITING IN VAIN

Words and Music by Bob Marley

I don't wanna wait in vain for your love.
I don't wanna wait in vain for your love.
From the very first time I blessed my eyes on you, girl,
My heart says, "Follow through."
But I know now that I'm way down on your line,
But the waiting feel is fine.
So don't treat me like a puppet on a string,
'Cause I know how to do my thing.
Don't talk to me as if you think I'm dumb.
I wanna know when you're gonna come.

See, I don't wanna wait in vain for your love.
I don't wanna wait in vain for your love.
I don't wanna wait in vain for your love.
'Cause it's summer is here,
I'm still waiting there.
Winter is here and I'm still waiting there.
Like I said,
It's been three years since I'm knockin' on your door,
And I still can knock some more.
Ooh, girl, ooh, girl,
Is it feasible, I wanna know now,
For I to knock some more?

Ya see, in life I know there is lots of grief,
But your love is my relief.
Tears in my eyes burn,
Tears in my eyes burn while I'm waiting,
While I'm waiting for my turn.

See, I don't wanna wait in vain for your love.
I don't wanna wait in vain for your love.
I don't wanna wait in vain for your love.
I don't wanna wait in vain for your love.
I don't wanna wait in vain for your love.
Oh, I don't wanna, I don't wanna,
I don't wanna, I don't wanna,
I don't wanna wait in vain.
No, I don't wanna, I don't wanna,
I don't wanna, I don't wannna,
I don't wanna wait in vain.

It's your love that I'm waiting on.
It's my love that you're running from.
(Repeat)

WAITING IN VAIN

Words and Music by
BOB MARLEY

REDEMPTION SONG

Words and Music by Bob Marley

Old pirates, yes, they rob I.
Sold I to the merchant ships
*   minutes after they took I from the bottomless pit.*
But my hand was made strong
*   by the hand of the Almighty.*
We forward in this generation triumphantly.

Chorus
Won't you help to sing these songs of freedom?
'Cause all I ever had, redemption songs,
*   redemption songs.*

Emancipate yourselves from mental slavery,
None but ourselves can free our minds.
Have no fear for atomic energy,
'Cause none of them can stop the time.
How long shall they kill our prophets
While we stand aside and look?
Yes, some say it's just a part of it.
We've got to fulfill the book.

To Chorus

Emancipate yourselves from mental slavery,
None but ourselves can free our minds.
Have no fear for atomic energy,
'Cause none of them can stop the time.
How long shall they kill our prophets
While we stand aside and look?
Yes, some say it's just a part of it.
We've got to fulfill the book.

Won't you help to sing these songs of freedom?
'Cause all I ever had, redemption songs,
All I ever had, redemption songs,
These songs of freedom, songs of freedom.

REDEMPTION SONG

Words and Music by
BOB MARLEY

SATISFY MY SOUL

Words and Music by Bob Marley

Oh please don't you rock my boat
Cause I don't want my boat to be rockin'.
Oh please don't you rock my boat no, no
Cause I don't want my boat to be rockin'.
I'm tellin you that oh, oh, wo, wo, wo, wo
I like it like it like this
So keep it stiff like this.

And you should know, you should know by now
I like it I like it like this.
I like it like this, ooh yeah.
You satisfy my soul, satisfy my soul
You satisfy my soul, satisfy my soul
Every little action, there's a reaction
Oh can't you see what you've done for me.
I'm happy inside all, all of the time.

When we bend a new corner I feel like a sweepstake winner
When I meet you around the corner you make me feel like a
sweepstake winner.
Can't you see? You must believe me.

Oh darling, darling, I'm calling, calling.
Can't you see? Why won't you believe me?
Oh darling, darling, I'm calling, calling.

When I meet you around the corner,
Oh I said, baby never let me be alone
And then you hold me tight, you make me feel alright
Yes, when you hold me tight, you make me feel alright.

Can't you see? Don't you believe me?
Oh darling, darling, I'm calling, calling.
Can't you see? Why won't you believe me?
Oh darling, darling, I'm calling, calling.
.

Satisfy my soul, satisfy my soul...
That's all I want to do,
That's all I'll take from you.

SATISFY MY SOUL

Words and Music by
BOB MARLEY

EXODUS
Words and Music by Bob Marley

Exodus, movement of Jah people, oh yeah.
Open your eyes and let me tell you this.

Men and people will fight ya down (Tell me why?)
 when ya see Jah light.
Let me tell you, if you're not wrong (Then why?)
 ev'rything is alright.
So we gonna walk, alright, through the roads of creation.
We're the generation (Tell me why.)
 trod through great tribulation.

Exodus, movement of Jah people.
Exodus, movement of Jah people.

Open your eyes and look within.
Are you satisfied with the life you're living?
We know where we're going; we know where we're from.
We're leaving Babylon, we're going to our fatherland.

Exodus, movement of Jah people.
(Movement of Jah people.)
Send us another Brother Moses gonna cross the Red Sea.
(Movement of Jah people.)
Send us another Brother Moses gonna cross the Red Sea.

Exodus, movement of Jah people.
Exodus, Exodus, Exodus, Exodus,
Exodus, Exodus, Exodus, Exodus.
Move! Move! Move! Move! Move! Move!

Open your eyes and look within.
Are you satisfied with the life you're living?
We know where we're going; we know where we're from.
We're leaving Babylon, we're going to the fatherland.

Exodus, movement of Jah people.
Exodus, movement of Jah people.
Movement of Jah people. (4 times)
Move! Move! Move! Move! Move! Move! Move!

Jah come to break down 'pression, rule equality,
Wipe away transgression, set the captives free.

Exodus, movement of Jah people.
Exodus, movement of Jah people.
Movement of Jah people. (5 times)

Move! Move! Move! Move! Move! Move!
Movement of Jah people. (5 times)

EXODUS

Strum Pattern 4
Moderate Reggae

Words and Music by
BOB MARLEY

Ex - o - dus, ___

move - ment of Jah peo - ple, oh ___

___ yeah. ___ O - pen your eyes and let me

83

85

set the cap - tives free. ___ Ex - o - dus, ___

move - ment of Jah peo -

- ple.

Repeat and Fade

Move - ment of Jah peo - ple;

JAMMING

Words and Music by Bob Marley

Ooh, yeah; well, alright.
We're jammin'.
I wanna jam it with you.
We're jammin', jammin',
And I hope you like jammin', too.
Ain't no rules, ain't no vow,
We can do it anyhow.
I and I will see you through.
'Cause every day we pay the price.
We are the living sacrifice,
Jammin' till the jam is through.

We're jammin'.
To think that jammin' was a thing of
  the past.
We're jammin',
And I hope this jam is gonna last.
No bullet can stop us now,
We neither beg nor we won't bow.
Neither can be bought nor sold.
We all defend the right,
Jah Jah children must unite,
For life is worth much more than gold.

We're jammin', jammin', jammin',
  jammin'.
And we're jammin' in the name of the
  Lord.
We're jammin', jammin', jammin',
  jammin'.
We're jammin' right straight from yard.
Singing Holy Mount Zion, Holy Mount
  Zion.
Jah sitteth in Mount Zion and rules all
  creation.
Yeah, we're jammin'. Bop-chu-wa-wa-wa.

We're jammin'.
I wanna jam it with you.
We're jammin', jammin', jammin',
  jammin'.
And Jamdown hope you're jammin', too.
Jah knows how much I 'ave tried.
The truth cannot hide
To keep you satisfied.
True love that now exists
Is the love I can't resist,
So jam by my side.

We're jammin', jammin', jammin',
  jammin'.
I wanna jam it with you.
We're jammin', we're jammin', we're
  jammin', we're jammin',
We're jammin', we're jammin', we're
  jammin', we're jammin'.
Hope you like jammin', too.
(Repeat)

JAMMING

Words and Music by
BOB MARLEY

USING THE STRUM PATTERNS

The songs in this book include suggested strum patterns (Strum Pattern 1.) for guitar. These numbers refer to the numbered strum patterns below.

The strumming notation uses special symbols to indicate up and down strokes.

$$\sqcap = \text{DOWN}$$

$$\text{V} = \text{UP}$$

Feel free to experiment with these basic patterns to create your own rhythmic accompaniment.

STRUM PATTERNS

Note: When an (x) is indicated in the pattern, mute the strings.

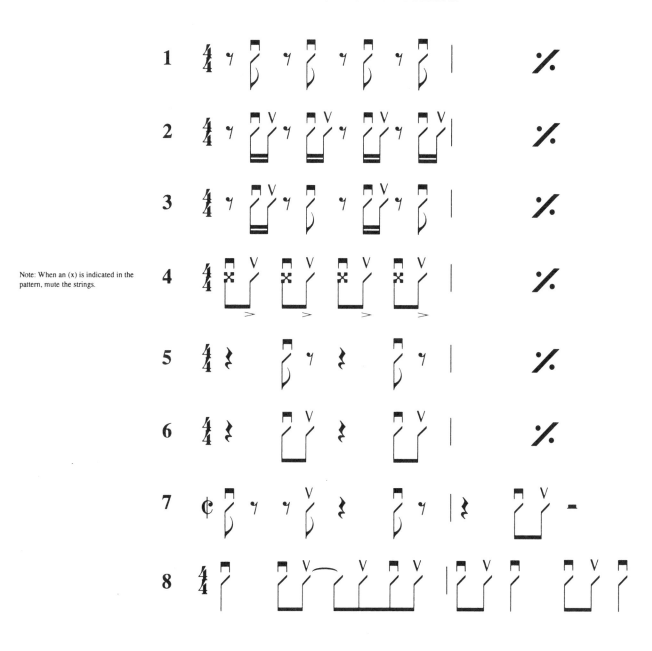